FEAR

S. E. McKenzie

S. E. MCKENZIE

FEAR

DEDICATION
To everyone who has been left out in the cold.

S. E. MCKENZIE

FEAR

TABLE OF CONTENTS

S. E. MCKENZIE

FEAR

FEAR

FEAR

I

So alone
In the Negative Zone
Fearing those they do not know

Cramped in the city
Squashed together.
No room to breathe.

Fear;
We feel it
Year after year.

We know the cost;
Tear after tear.
We don't know how to count what is lost.

Beautiful Child
Depends on love
And a gentle touch.

Close your eyes now
For War Time is on Parade;
To win one must know how to degrade.

S. E. MCKENZIE

I see the hope in your eyes;
Beautiful Child;
What will this fog of war leave behind for you?

And no war is holier than your innocence.
Oh Beautiful Child
What will be left for you?

Small town one percent
Never caring about informed consent
As long as they can gouge you in your rent.

II

Oh Beautiful Child
What shall we keep
Your destiny is shaped while you sleep.

Subtle fear of loss can grow violent in the mind;
Can make many unkind;
So willing to be willfully blind.

Oh Beautiful Child, you have no past to leave behind;
While the weapons of war degrade
Seem to always be on parade.

FEAR

Mis-leaders attached to opposing books
They are always quick to judge those
On looks.

They pray to the thing;
They hope for the thing;
They fight for the thing.

And once the battle is won;
The thing rusts and fades away;
Never able to stay for another day.

Timocracy;
Descendants of a noble aristocracy;
Froze social mobility;

So long ago.
No turning point;
No entry point;

Very few would know;
Out of sight
Was out of mind

S. E. MCKENZIE

Inferior nature
Of Timocrats
Made it so.

Social Power
Deriving from wealth
A long time ago.

Monetized matter too.

But below the ground
Invisible forces were raging
The Timocrats were too narrow minded

To see
For they were only descendants
Of a noble aristocracy.

Timocrats
Born into wealth
Which gave them power

From birth
This is how
They valued their worth.

FEAR

Negative Social Reproduction
Closed doors
Of schools

Fools
Hoped
To rule fools.

The one percent and their wanna bees
Swarm around their chosen one.
See how they hate

While shaping her fate;
Too hardened to change their minds.
Now for Louise it is too late.

The deed has been done;
They group like beasts
As they mark their feast.

Negative Social Reproduction
Frozen in Time
No turning point; no entry point;

S. E. MCKENZIE

Steely rigid Timocrats;
So top heavy;
Could not move forward;

Descendants of a noble aristocracy
Never needing to grow
Never needing to know

The other side of the universe.
Timeless forces
Earth, Water and Fire;

Sky power;
Electrifying;
Terrifying;

The source of Nature's force
They could never see;
They could never be;

Even if they wanted to.
Too much fright
Paralyzed what could have been might.

FEAR

The Timocracy
Were fools
Needing fools to rule.

Oh see Fear entice;
See Fear pretending to be nice;
See Fear and its cost;

Innocence is now lost.

See Fear in their face;
See Fear all over the place.
In this world too afraid to love.

Big bucks to be made
In war and gloom,
Love is free and there is never enough.

Love knows that Peace
Could never come too soon
In this land of gloom and doom.

So many turn away
Not knowing what to say
While the Beautiful Child

Has nowhere to play.
The world is on the brink
Of war; some are driven to drink;

Others don't know what to think.

III

Oh how Louise grew
Until she could not fit
Into the pigeon hole

Anymore;
All the gatekeepers made sure
That the door was always closed to her;

Unless she paid a professional assessor
$1.5 K
To stay

Connected
And to be educated
To a higher degree;

Otherwise
She would have no
Opportunity;

FEAR

Accept drinks that were free.
Days were buried into the past
Rather fast.

She could not find a place she could afford to keep;
So she had nowhere to sleep;
While every door was being slammed in her face.

There was nowhere she could belong;
Not one single place
To call her own. Louise was all alone.

IV

There was a place
Across the sea
And far away

Where we were told the war was about Liberty;
We were told what to fear and what to kill.
We were not shown the blood and gore,

S. E. MCKENZIE

Though we had heard about it all before,
We didn't know what we were fighting for.
Very few could listen;

And very few could see;
The rarest freedom of all
Is to be the best you can be.

Sharing the same host
A planet so blue
We were all brothers and sisters

And life was our glue.
We were stuck together
In a system of unity

That we could not see
And the greatest freedom of all
Was to stay real during the Fall.

To never be defined;
Defiled;
Captured by negativity's pull;

FEAR

And lost in Eternity's Wind.

The war was very far away across the sea;
We were told
That we must fight for Liberty.

And Big Brother told us who was mentally ill;
And who to fear;
Who to shun when they were near.

Oh Beautiful Child
Still so small
Living behind the wall

He shows so much love.
He feeds on love.
He becomes that love.

V

Oh the lead man
How he could plan.
And he knew

That he could unite
And delight
After the Demise of Louise;

S. E. MCKENZIE

She would not recover from her latest fright;
Which lasted all night;
Everyone said that it wasn't right;

But the villain was let go
And was no longer in sight.
He had tasted blood

And felt his might
Now the little man
Felt like a big man.

Dirty Politics; Shitily Managed;
Win any way you can
Makes a little man feel like a big man.

Let him smirk
While he jerks
Going to work.

Defame;
Slander her name;
Manufacture consent;

FEAR

Pretend that you are a member
Of the one percent;
Entitled to bring anyone down;

Blank face now wearing a frown.

To shape intent so criminal
Into something appearing more civil;
So a little man can feel like a big man.

How did Hitler Rise?
Was he living
Behind a disguise?

While he generated Fear
And absolute control
How could he have been like that?

What hurt him so bad?
What made him so mad?
Imagine what could have been

S. E. MCKENZIE

If peace had been given the chance
It needed to grow
From today into tomorrow.

Timocrat could not be criticized;
He was just a little man
Wanting to feel like a big man.

Dirty Politics; Shitily Managed;

He will need someone even smaller
To shout at;
Dirty Politics; Shitily Managed;

Get what you can;
So the little man
Can feel like a big man.

Big brother announced her name;
Helped to degrade the woman behind the door;
So that attacking her became fair game;

FEAR

Less than criminal now;
For everyone said
That they knew all about her;

Though they never knew her at all
For she was living behind
A make-shift wall.

And the evil tone;
Echoed through the Negative Zone.
When Louise was all alone.

Big Brother was watching
Through the eye
In the sky.

He didn't shed a tear
He didn't cry
He began to believe the lie.

Now it was said all knew her;
And the little man who wanted to be a big man
Never questioned the lie

S. E. MCKENZIE

Even when his cruelty made her cry
And made him a lesser man
Than he could have been.

So the lead man,
With the plan,
Realized quite soon

How popular it would be
To study
The sad Demise of Louise.

The same system that overcharged
For an assessment
To keep her connected

And educated to a higher degree
Did not connect the dots
That could no longer move

On Scatter Plots
But any conclusion would do
For the study would be read by very few

FEAR

The pay would make them middle class;
The Pull of feeling elite;
Treating others as if they were living on the street.

Yes that was the way
To raise the ceiling
And it seemed to be so appealing.

A good rant
Would get a large government grant
Much more

Than the cost of the assessment
That could have kept Louise connected.
But the connection was lost

Like a broken telephone
Leaving Louise totally alone
In a world where they refused to hear her speak.

A cyber leak was free to tell the truth
Big Brother said Louise was known,
Though there was no proof to be shown.

S. E. MCKENZIE

Not even a call to verify
Whether this conclusion
Was just another lie.

Dirty Politics; Shitily managed;
For the evidence was locked
Out of sight.

Behind a door
Nothing new;
Just be glad it didn't happen to you.

And a third world war
Was rumored to be flaming
Across the sea

But no one could see;
What was happening here;
The lack of value was clear;

The cost made them fear
The war that was so far away
Could one day be here.

FEAR

But not today;
And big brother said
Louise knew who killed her.

But if she really knew him
I know she would have ran away.
I knew it was true

Big Brother was manufacturing consent
Again
As a member of the one percent.

Watch the empty street
So many are gone
Just vanished

They are now half alive behind a wall

Very few
Knew them
At all.

Now Time has gone
World's opportunities closed
To too many;

S. E. MCKENZIE

While the robo-beast
Surveys
Without a word;

To satisfy the one percent
While manufacturing consent
To be disenfranchised and to be left alone;

Free from pain but never free;
Pushing Louise out of society;
Dirty Politics; Shitily Managed;

In the poorest part of town
No longer designed
For smooth market flow;

Designed as a place
For the Nouveau Poor
To go.

Pretty barriers to channel
Those in cars
To drive past fast.

FEAR

No longer middle class.

The cop on the beat
Stared at Louise
As if she was living on the street.

No one remembers the day
Before the barriers
Transformed our Right of Way.

Barriers;
To channel the well to do
To drive away.

Barriers;
Called a thing of beauty
Silently doing their duty.

And Big Brother said
He knew them all;
As privacy rights vanished too.

No manual controls;
Just automated;
Water too hot

S. E. MCKENZIE

And water too cold;
Will always be that way
While you grow old.

Chaos;

So the little man can feel like a big man;
He manufactures consent
There is nothing he needs to prevent.

Later; time and evidence would fade;
While big war machines so ready to kill
Were put on parade to give Joe Public a thrill.

Sometimes the wounded are killed
By mistake;
It is hard to know what is made up and fake.

No reason for Big Brother
To repent;
He is part of the one percent.

Little man
Now feels like a big man
After he manufactures consent

FEAR

One more time again.
He could never win
On a level playing field.

The little man
Lets hate
Control fate

While looking for people all alone;
Their world soon to be turned upside down;
The glass ceiling

Becomes the floor
Just like the way it is done
Many times before.

Oh Beautiful Child
Do not forget who you are;
You are the Son of War.

As Big Brother yanks the chain.
The Demise of Louise
Is hidden under the cover;

S. E. MCKENZIE

Owned by Big Brother.
Just another energy vampire;
Roaming; lost in his pride;

There is nowhere to hide
When you are all alone
Walking in the Negative Zone.

Mean Girls will look so nice
Mean Boys will be as cold as ice.
You; Beautiful Child;

Remember who you are;
You are the Son of War;
Maybe the worst war we have ever had;

Don't feel sad
Don't feel bad
Remember who you are

You are the Son of War.

THE END

FEAR

Produced by S.E. McKenzie Productions
First Print Edition October 2015

S. E. MCKENZIE

Enquiries: 1(778)992-2453
Mailing Address:
S. E. McKenzie Productions
168 B 5th St.
Courtenay, BC
V9N 1J4

Email Address: messidartha@aol.com

http://www.amazon.com/SarahMcKenzie/e/B00H9RWX48
/ref=ntt_dp_epwbk_0

www.ingramcontent.com/pod-product-compliance
Lightning Source LLC
Chambersburg PA
CBHW060548030426
42337CB00021B/4488